The Oblong Plot

The Oblong Plot

Chris Andrews

PUNCHER & WATTMANN

First published in 2024
Published by Puncher & Wattmann
PO Box 279
Waratah NSW 2298

info@puncherandwattmann.com

NATIONAL
LIBRARY
OF AUSTRALIA

A catologue record for this book is available from The National Library of Australia.

ISBN   9781923099173

Cover Photograph : Joy M. Lai, '9:36pm. Last Drinks, Eora Land, Sydney, Australia', from the *Nighthawks* series
Cover design by David Musgrave
Printed by Lightning Source International

for my sister, Jan

Contents

Pacific Rim

To a lone tourist at a loose end
in this city of funiculars
a sprayed wall says: *Lift your head Princess,
your crown's about to fall*. There's a dog
asleep in a thicket of footsteps,
a boarded-up Palace of Rubber,
and a well-presented man who rides
the microbuses tenaciously
expounding the merits of a comb.

It's the evening of the holiday,
and the people, whether built for pain
or giggles, crowd the foreshore to watch
the gold sovereign drop into the slot
and bring on the slow train of starlight.
A bath toy famously lost at sea
fetches up bleached and incognito.
Lavish foam of the swash comes seething
in over the ragged backwash foam.

There's a stack of Hanjin containers
painted a red that goes on glowing
deep into dusk, an almost empty
artspace in a disappearing jail,
a fuchsia riot, a hummingbird's
precision sipping, and a mother
of infant twins who used to be glad
of her gift for deep sleep downloading
a seismograph app for her smartphone.

Under Fang

Day my colour-bound myopia,
before you go can I just say how
claret leaves cut puzzles in the blue
and what the skywriter hearted there
was anybody's progressive guess.
Day the only place for us to park
our demountable utopia,
don't slip away like a timid guest
before I can say just how you go.

Another brilliant day gone missing
the never-yet-assembled fragments,
with nothing to guide me but the ghost
of a pattern: net trap set to catch
the matter that could make a part whole.
Rumbly bins, Venus dipping to kiss
lichen-crusted tiles, and here you are:
dusk my shot of myalgia my
shadow-flooded topiary maze.

It might be true, what my brother says:
I like to aim low. My ambition:
to remain an opsimath. Success:
not having quite given up just yet.
But I stand under a blown street lamp.
It's Alphard, so my phone-eye tells me,
at the far end of the starlight thread.
Somebody watching under you, Fang.
Deep sky night my ache my opiate.

different / same

spongy buffalo
lawn mown short

palm beard muttering
rust edge sky

reach for the orange
brick still warm

parching and drenching
shoe strung high

black chip enamel
tea gone cool

fierce little fist raised
girl brought home

depthless perception
flat blur still

everything / nothing
different / same

green fleck laminex
mint fresh coin

dozing and leaking
song sung low

toenail nemesis
sheet worn thin

tentative tendril
hook flung slow

adamant hunger
cut sewn tight

never / forever
no time / soon

Monday remember
chip shop shut

ghostly echidna
five cent moon

The Jennifer

Arthur last seen at a posh college
dealing ironically: first to go.
The David who wore out his supports
and said, while I tried not to fidget,
'They'll share their words of wisdom, even
give you money, but time? Not so much.'
Louise who discovered a talent
for big and dirty simulations.
Paula with her capital of cool.

Anil who was simply the quickest.
The Jennifer with contact lenses
who two or three times was naturally
curious to see if alcohol
would go on opening up the world
and has never remembered slurring,
'WE are going to be girlz forEVVA,'
stretched out on the back seat of the bus.
Some years down the track her speech is crisp:

'Jesus, I can't even shit in peace.'
And: 'They're all so frank and generous
with advice, but not with help, as such.'
Then she chuckles and is on her feet
before I hear the crying begin.
The ghost of a netted mango tree
presiding over her concrete yard.
A festive mist of katydid clinks.
The Ken who played the harp. Bright Arthur.

I Was There

I saw mangroves comb the river bend
for plastic, and the dazzle-point slide
on a ripple of pelican wake.
I saw razor scooters left to rust.
The simple rules of the Game of Life
played out into wonderland: I saw
some powerful minds narrow the quest
for the smallest Garden of Eden
to a ten-by-ten-cell bounding box.

I saw the Y2K bug fizzle
and the flourishing of martyrdom.
Venus was a tiny mobile mole
on the face of the sun. I was there:
she who never says anything said,
'I want this minuted. Since boasting
is such a big part of what we do,
we can hardly be expected not
to boast about how well we do it.'

I saw the wheels of fashion grinding
(they were *exasperatingly* slow).
I did see some hard-eyed realists
who had politely repressed a smile
when we declined to get with the strength
abandoned by their meltaway real
(if I forget that, step on my toes).
I saw hypnotic splotches of paint,
and deep cuts in a veteran sawhorse.

Broken List

A headland rears its painterly bulk.
The carpark is sprinkled with brown glass.

Here for a few more years is the wall
of a jail, blank as the bay is long.

A sole wisp of cloud wrings itself dry.
Only so many rides on the wave.

Anger is out there looking for fuel.
There is a poison that never spoils.

The inlet fills up like a slow lung.
A downward-drawn whorl spools off the oar.

How deep the night is, how sad the cries
of a plover pair, depends, depends.

A padlock rusts. A wedding ring sinks.
A child tries on a costume of kelp.

Here is a man who wondered how long
he would have to wait outside the law.

A coal ship lifts off the horizon.
Haze blurs the lighthouse on its cream plinth.

I remember a spell to reverse
the spiral of the inward-drawn I.

Plovers call. So much depends upon
where a name fell on a broken list.

The inlet is spilling now: listen.
The ocean is dark heave and tinsel.

Water that has never fallen still
will never say, Best line: be silent.

A leg hangs from a low-slung hammock.
A bell spreads its invisible rings.

The Balconies

Of the pods that cling to this brick cliff
no two hold the same: here succulents,
there an ashtray in austere exile.
One tenant's temporary slumming,
another's dream of independence
in three small rooms and a balcony
with a gappy breeze-block parapet.
A dream that fades but slowly, gently
over months of stepping out to gaze

up at sassy cockatoos or down
at the tea that brews in a dinghy
on a chained trailer with two flat tyres.
There a neglected punching bag, here
mint in fitted styrofoam planters
dripping brightly. When night washes in
lit by the chilly glow of plasma
or the ardour of barbecue coals,
feet fall asleep in sisterly hands.

To one who saw the removalists
as agents of intimate ruin,
the dun hue of these sun-hiving bricks
is the amber that stills a moment:
it was a move that had worked before
but never quite like this: she reached out
with a clear enough sense of the worst
that could happen, fluently, bold as
bougainvillea claiming a lane.

Out of There

She used a five-cent coin to remove
the slightly rusted thumbtacks holding
two photos to the soft partition
(grizzled dog with cloudy eyes at rest,
granite-shadow volumes in a cwm),
placed them in the open farewell card,
and reread a pair of inscriptions:
'You're going to miss us but remember
a molecule's always there for you.'

'The Wonders of the World are waiting
to fill the backgrounds of your selfies.'
To the question, 'Are you sure you want
to delete ... ?' she kept answering yes
as the corners of the open plan
emptied one by one. With thumb held out
and a swivel of the wrist she made
a sign that meant *We'll set up a drink*
to a colleague walking out the door.

Left alone, she put on the headset,
recorded a new call-queue message:
'We're sorry to keep you waiting but
it doesn't pay to meet peak demand,'
rubbed the small of her back, hit erase,
launched the text-to-speech synthesizer,
flexed her fingers, and typed: 'This system
was not designed to waste human lives
but humans built every part of it.'

My Day For Spilling Things

Ibises flying. I wake and taste
the dust that has settled on my tongue.
Supplementary test your time starts now,
I thought the radio said before
the ancient dream invigilator
came to snatch away the magic bloc.
There's a little patch of yellow wall:
fresh sunlight nesting in an air vent.
Qantas is flying. I drink and break
the drought that was reaching down my throat.
For a blink I feel I'm what the book
I was reading when I fell asleep
was about: the heretical hunch
that you and I and the girl I saw
giving everyone on the ferry
and nobody special the finger
are moments in the universe's
gradual waking up to itself.
Coffee filters. I sip it and wake
a window on the abyss of bits.
News feeds hunger for things that go bang:
celebrity groin, checkpoint blunder.
This is how they learn what FRAG OUT means
where the rate of watercourse repair
depends so much on a wheelbarrow.
Qanats are flowing. They split and spread
an aquifer's cool bounty around.
While docile library rats are trained
to brag about their global impact,
avalanches of sludge pour over
the edge of the continental shelf,
and arsenal engineers take pride
in the high fragment penetration

of a widely bootlegged hand grenade.
Emirates flying. You bite the toast.
Curtain rings clack together and there:
plumbago blossom glows in the dim,
datura plays its fanfare downwards.
Russet pelt, black angles: a fox flew
to where its weathering carcass hangs
against the rose and pink constructions
of cumulus puffing itself up
from mediocris to congestus.
Airbuses lumber. I take and waste
a fraction of the time that remains.
Urban bulbuls with red whiskers sing
in a potted pomegranate tree.
I count the jolts of a long coal train
and bits of a misremembered song
stutter up from the root of the tongue.

YaTube

No marble immobility, I
don't always *have* to be CONVULSIVE.
I can move like the lips of a sphinx,
too slowly for human eyes, or wait
like undeciphered script on a plinth.
I'm all the years of pfaffing around
that had to go into the album
of luxuriant plunderphonics
generations gave up waiting for.

Say meh but I'll already be gone.
Anywhere is the true phantom site.
In the house of an imposter aunt
I hear what the piano mutters:
the lost name of the mason whose hand
earnestly grasped the chisel that cut
the words *writ in Water* into stone.
I'm a sum of atom units. I'm
a microbe nation. Pain tutors me.

When everything seems put to remain,
I'm the absent hammer holding off.
My other name is importunate.
I crack open the puritan tome
to extract the utopian terms:
riot map, opium tune, net star.
I love the movement that displaces
the lines. This might sound up itself but
I knew you'd find me. And here you are.

Street of Thirsty Boats

Beautiful how stubbornly some parts
of a dying organism heal
right up to the general collapse
as if to imply: what short of all
there is could really count as a whole?
Or that's what a person in rude health
might think before the pain graph ticks up.
How thoughtful of you algorithm
to show me people clutching their guts.

How sweet to remember my birthday.
Oracle Ana says: 'The live stream
would like to be your evil master.'
No you do not have my attention,
hypnoscreen. I want the news of here,
the word on the street of thirsty boats,
shining even as showers mop Earlwood.
Skink generation come out and bask.
Cough softly cat with a too-big heart.

Stubbornly two mynahs keep plucking
at the flattened carcass of a third,
lifting it momentarily back
into the air, as if to reply:
This part of us, fallen, this whole part.
Boot pegs scale a leaning public pole
into deep cyanic shades of air:
escape routes in every direction.
Faint away rainbow fragment. Stay ghost.

Ten Bels

What if they hadn't slowed on a whim
for that gently lifting exit ramp
and then for the ferny hairpin bends
of the road down to the deep-set bay?

When they pulled up and broke the door-seal
their private hit of spring on repeat
laying the groundwork for nostalgia
was swallowed by a great wall of sound:
the ten-bel din of massed cicadas.

A dune had spilt into the carpark.
The mustard façade of the hotel
was peeling around a FOR SALE sign.
Out the back, jacarandas billowed.

They might have been drawn to the café
with its tall windows standing open
and never set foot in that dim bar
where the long conversation began,
no rush to lay out the conditions.

When the sun fell behind the charred head
and the double drummers quit popping,
they came out to sit on cooling sand
and pioneering stems of pigface.
Lengthening bars of foam gathered up
what was left of light below. Above,
a buff tower of cloud was topping out.

Behind them, in town, gardenias
were mounting a blossom offensive.
A new kind of night was opening:

neither casino nor museum
of morbid reconstructions. The life
spread before them like green mustard fields
over the great divide would begin
with a room at the Criterion
that time had ignored: doilies, valet,
tallboy, jug cover, lush ceiling rose.

Moments before the bottom dropped out
of the storm, a soft bluish crackle
between microfibre and gooseflesh.

They woke to the flavour of a dream
gone except that all was forgiven
and looked down at the rented sedan
carpeted with Tyrian purple.

The exoskeleton of a nymph
exploded but clinging emptily
was there to tell them: No going back.

What if they hadn't enquired within
and opened the box of the question:
If this is happiness, what was that?

They might have been spared a phantom ache
but it was still better to have known
the original Criterion.

Dinky File

I'm warning you now: it could happen.
So many stronger, brighter young things
set forth gaily, sure of possessing
some kind of indomitable core.
They thought irony would protect them.
How could they not underestimate
what time would do with its dinky file?
But how could they have reached the front door,
knowing they were beaten already?

If it happens, there will be no time.
Don't even think about gathering
a few treasured possessions. Just go.
Forget the black-and-white photograph
of a girl stroking a dog long gone
in a garden buried by cement
in a country that doesn't exist.
The red tape reduction committee
is debating its terms of reference.

I need a KPI to measure
progress towards my personal goal
of caring less what the big man thinks.
If I use the word *impactful*, if
I give up the long and subtle art
of disappointing, if I forget
curriculum's a diminutive,
it means I've already been bitten
and there's nothing anyone can do.

Swap

'You really need to clean this bag out,
Sunshine,' said the smiling constable.
The red neon TAX sign flickered on.
The charity bin was choking full.
'And what is this?' he asked, extracting
a metal box with buttons and knobs.
His baseball cap was silhouetted
against a space of indigo air
freshly outlined by scaffolding pipes.

'A Biscuit.' 'Right.' 'No, it is. I mean ...'
Coal train screeching. Currawong exchange.
The grim senior constable returned
with my license. A minimal jerk
of her chin meant, *Give him back his toy*.
Disappointingly clean, I watched them
lurch away in their tactical pants.
The plane trees in the rackety wilds
of the railway corridor fluttered.

An oblique path through the dim forest
of letters led to the very word
at which the force had cut in, but soon
my friend with the Tetra was smiling
down through the windscreen. 'I know, I saw,
but hey,' she said, a little swivel
of her eyes drawing a line from rust
up to a weather-beaten sneaker
spinning beside a cable-cut moon.

Fallen Star

There I am on the kerb.
Night-ingot glides over.

Smooth limo-driver smiles:
my tyres are mystery.

From the dim ember-cave
comes a voice: Share my ride?

Long hair loose, no face work,
legendary giggle,

the calm fallen star winks:
My rise was misery.

Licensed boors telling me:
I can break what I made.

What did they ever make?
Bubbles pop anyway.

Streamy-eyed gurus all
my-stare-is-mastery.

What was that? Wisdom or
wise-sounding wiliness?

There I go blethering.
What are you working on?

(Short pause while I wonder
what she could possibly?)

Turn it up, Efraín!
It's that East Islander.

A&R know-it-alls
didn't hear this coming.

Kid on a hit roll sings
my lode is melody.

What stone was it under,
that simple arrangement?

Simple now but the world
had to grow a new ear.

Kid had to copy wrong.
Queen of the meme error.

Now I'm a stay-at-home,
my Rome is memory:

ready-lost paradise,
door ajar for the gone.

What Ana Says

In the darkening plaza I find
her place taped off and dug up. A child
catches my eye and points: there she is
in a doorway with her letter tiles.
It's oddly quiet: no starlings yet.
With a go-thither glare, Ana says:
'Good evening, Mr. Pleased with Himself
for having discovered what millions
never had permission not to know.

If you were hoping for something clear
you should have been patient and waited
in the cartomancer's spiral queue.
If you think you wish everyone well,
beware the team for cultural change.
Beware the lilly-pilly bearings.
If you think the words you're using now
are safe from becoming offensive,
it's time you bit the too-hard biscuit.'

Ana says: 'A twitter renown is
only sort of written on water.
Call that protracted twitching patience?
Stamp those wee boots, Mr. Baby Grey.
You were thrown, so throw yourself. Begin
again with what there is: this weather,
the dark murmuration descending.
Too late is way later than you'd like.
The last waking thought is a jetty.'

The Backhouses

Spica pinned bright and cool over Mars.
Among the names of the unreturned,
cut into dark granite and gilded,
five Backhouses. The Peace Garden drips:
the roses are blown, the petals strewn.
An open car glides by declaring:
My driver may not magnetize but
you shall feel the thumping of my subs
in the cage where every song begins.

The club is drawing a crowd tonight.
In the 'Japanese-inspired' courtyard,
a teenager squints into the pond,
searching for an old tea-coloured koi.
The talks many thought impossible
have begun, or so a ticker says
on a decorative TV screen,
but it won't be over till the men
with the squat pens sign. And even then.

There's a glut of muscle. Repartee
and nonchalance landed this bouncer
his job, and he's right: it's bye-byes time,
but the drunk is broke, the taxi flown.
The returned serviceman at the bar
is a bit wobbly on his pins too
but firm in his belief that the quest
won't even begin until the kid
with the fat glasses gets up to sing.

The Tyranny of Quirks

In the lost masterwork of Melbourne fumblecore
set in the summer when the shuffle met the bounce,
there are hesitations so patiently rehearsed
you'd swear the actors were winging it or blanking.
The whole stunt / accident distinction collapses
in an unspectacular way on the dancefloor,
any surface, that is, with the requisite slip.
Microphones got buried in leisurewear, so when
from the depths of hood and couch our lost heroine
sums up the lesson of the seminar, it sounds
like stuttering: 'Posers of posers are posers.'
One review was titled, 'The Tyranny of Quirks.'
The one. I'm not saying it was hard to be snide
about those nicely put-together young people
savouring the privilege of disillusion
in a world where most don't even get what it was
they thought they wanted. But I have not forgotten
a scene singled out for its sheer self-indulgence:
Who is this not even secondary character
puttering wearily amid party jetsam,
purging ash and dregs, momentarily tempted
by thimblefuls of distillate but saved by yawns,
while a far magpie descants, and the light balance
tips imperceptibly from lamp to paling sky?
And another scene, dismissed as 'decoration':
a man comes up the street in a wheelchair shouting:
'I want to walk again. I want to *fucking walk*!'
and some nimble hand-held camera operating
shows how two tenants of the standard miracle
are broken in their strides and don't know where to look.

Honey Encryption

This line came to me out of the dark:
suspiciously luminous gherkin.
And then it was the promised iceberg,
an intern with his neurohammer,
midnight calm, a lake of tea, the south
with its barbaric clusters of stars ...
None of it made much sense but I thought:
If it's all there is in the pantry,
I can make the dark meal out of this.

My flame card is the key to the town.
Fire opens all the doors. There's a man
cut in half by a window growling:
'Another think coming if you think
this line can tame the dark out of me.'
In dreams begin repermutations
of everything from Aldebaran
down to the writhing compost of shames
the inner life makes a dark mouth eat.

And the light came out of this marquee
when a proboscis lifted the flap
and the glittery ringmaster barked:
Fame is the outer mark of decline.
Cucumber lamp, I hear your command
– Make the dim owl-star the key of night! –
in each fresh remash of the message
I've been failing to grasp ever since
this line came out of the dark at me.

The Returns

Old staples: But of course I can fly!
I keep my mouth shut because it's full
of loose teeth. And I'm mildly dismayed
to find a whole new room in the house.
Local variants: Lobsters for hands.
The friable slope that I must climb
is steepening to concavity.
Surprise mineralogy exam
with a hundred stained and greasy slides.

And every not so often, as if
to complement the dim business
of my dream capital, the return
of the Subalpine Crepuscular:
reaching the tree-line as daylight fails,
pressing on breathlessly to the lip
of an upland that heaves into view
and sweeps away: an undulant pound
darkening around patches of snow

and jaggedly rimmed. When the wind drops,
intricate trickling. On the far side,
dolerite columns rise from rubble
and break into a rose-flushed chaos
of blocks on the peak whose name is lost.
I should go back. I'm not dressed for this,
and the others will be worrying.
But there's something magnetic about
those weeping lenses of last year's snow.

The Island in the Roundabout

It was the coveted upstairs room
at the front, with a balcony, his
by virtue of seniority.
He went in, snatching things off the floor.
In that first, unforgotten moment
the space had a pre-electric depth:
a mirror's elliptical silver
swimming in the wardrobe's charcoal bulk.
The sash window showed how a street lamp
can gather a nest of glistening twigs.

What am I doing here? she wondered.
And: Who still has that many CDs?
He hesitated, hoping to choose
something that wouldn't be too over.
What I could do with a room like this!
she thought, mentally placing her things.
In hay-fever time, elm keys would swirl
on the balcony around a cup
of slow tea and her drying toenails,
and when exams were done, the others
would go back to Bendigo or Shep
or Wang or wherever and leave her
alone, luxuriously alone.
He came and put his hands on her hips.
She wouldn't have said it was over
that music; it had always been dull.
He was dancing her unhurriedly
towards the bed. He could dance. And talk.
He had gone to the big world out there
and come back with travel capital.

But he was a questioner as well.
Maybe she'd given away too much.
Her hands had already discovered
that he wasn't as thin as he looked.
With that moustache, he reminded her
of the well-oiled conjuring artist
in an ironic remake. The sky
from where she lay was still indigo
between branches and scaffolding pipes.
An arpeggiated major chord
carried from the station. When he ripped
the shiny plastic wrapper, she balked.
Not that it all had to be sublime.
She wouldn't have said he was creepy
(though she could imagine he might be
one day), just a bit too interested
in the whole first time thing. He sat up
and said there was no hurry, at all,
looking winded and tight in the face.
Then: 'Why would you like guys, anyway?'
There's an extrapolation, she thought.
And: Funny how people will not rest
until they have a box around you.
A molecule was still there for him:
he rummaged in a drawer and began
pinching, rolling, expertly licking.
There was no denying it: she too
had the spooky power to divert
the flow of somebody else's blood.
He jerked the squealing sash up and stepped
out onto the splintery grey boards.
After a moment's hesitation
she pulled her jumper on and followed.
There was a scent of pittosporum.
He had lifted his mini blow torch

when a squad car pulled up in the street.

Two officers in tactical pants
approached a car parked in the lamplight.
A tap on the window made the man
inside look up with a fading smile
from the book propped on the steering wheel.

Watching this scene unfold from above,
the artist conjured his joint away,
gave her shoulder a squeeze and whispered:
'Reading in a stationary vehicle:
ignorance of law is no excuse.'
The knot in his face had come undone.
A search of the reader's bag turned up
nothing but a metal box with knobs
the likes of which she had once seen deep
in the jungle of a studio.
There was only so long she could say:
Sex is something other people do.
But she had thought it often enough
to go on feeling that it would be,
that it was a kind of betrayal.

Thumb on fob, the senior constable
lifted her head to yawn and saw them:
the wild-haired kids on the balcony,
freshly disentangled, half their luck.
The boy was smiling. The girl's hand rose
as if to wave, then hovered and dropped.

Before her palm settled on the rail,
she saw it coming: as the squad car
glided away with submarine ease,
impeccably lubed, he turned, brows high,

head tilted, and said: 'Friend of the force?'
Maybe just then, in a way, she was
but, embarrassed, she had turned to look
at the island in the roundabout,
its three loose-limbed, lemon-scented gums
swaying almost imperceptibly.

Two Bridges

A fish plops back into the river.
A woman on the bridge who kisses
each slice of bread before she sends it
spinning away through the gnatty air.
The rake is set at a new angle
in its rain-pocked bunker, and the cars
idle over the incoming tide.
I believe what the scrum master says:
the future belongs to the agile.

I'm just not sure about agile: good.
A jackhammer jars its backhoe arm.
A wet demolition saw cuts in.
A crumpled youth interminably
tuning his ukulele beside
the cash machine, preparing to sing
for his ibuprofen is perhaps
the still middle-point of this ripping
up and down and out to fill the skips.

What if it's more agile to outsource
the enforcement of paralysis?
A man on the railway bridge who counts
rolls of steel. A student of English
as a third language eventually
inferring that *Ikn* means *I think*.
What carbs escape this ibis probing
will be discovered when brightness falls
and the netways of ratwork go live.

Glow Still

In the mansion of insomnia,
a door ajar. I pushed. It opened
onto the working sketch of a day.
Fawns of drop-cloth, sandpaper, sawdust.
A flipbook of swatches left behind
by painters called to another job.
Hessian the tone of cloud that comes down
to rest on a lake's replenished lens
and hide vast ranges of damp slate blue.

Week-old daffodil water the shade
of a rackety patch of sunlight
in the corner of a quadrangle
where a small thumb presses to release
a pungency of mandarin peel.
Kerosene cantaloupe the nuance
of dawn light climbing down from the tip
of a flexing Norfolk Island pine
(it's symmetry versus the sea wind).

A tumblerful of coloured thimbles.
A spattered sawhorse. Two stiff brushes.
It was the forever unfinished,
the space invisible on the plan,
the gap that allows the rest to move,
a luminosity spring by night,
by day a starlight impluvium,
the place of the shadow splice, and I
feel the glow still of that phantom site.

strange FM

what the fridge magnets said
vast fame and broken sight

order reigns by reorderings
listen to me stolen time

move things and breakfast
smoke vents and a bar fight

what's in the fridge: data gems
item: some little sonnet

weigh the dadaist fragments
fastest-moving handbrake

damages withstand the grief
lit memento stolen site

make soft and brave things
snake eats wolf is snowflake

Advanced Souvlaki

A kookaburra sits on the cage
at the top of the rusty stinkpole
with a neckless air of gravity.
A man with a spirit level trips.
The grandad caravan with its crown
of loudspeakers is back from Darwin.
If the question is still, What's the point
of anything at all? there's nothing
left to start to make an answer from.

Behind the cluttered yard that will be
three dark garage spaces for crickets
to stridulate in, a cottage squats.
The dead man's fingers are red in claw.
Pizza and scandalized reaction
are proffered in a mini-playground
with a massive sandstone portico.
It should have been abundantly clear
for some time now that you're with stupid.

It's the conference of the currawongs;
no ambulance can interrupt it.
Two fresh-faced Euro-canvassers tread
the narrow path to the hoarder's door.
In front of the gutted shop that was
Advanced Souvlaki, a rubber kid
tries his rabona kick on a stone
and ¡GOL! I can't fault those arguments
to justify despair. You know that.

Brother

People get us mixed up all the time
but if what nature really abhors
is uniformity, we're OK.
We look at a painting. Your gaze flies
to the vanishing point in the sun.
Mine sinks to the squishy fallen pear.
You wish people would open up more.
I think wait you can't unsee that stuff.
Where I spy a fathomless chasm

you find a slide on a gentle cline.
All around me, standards are falling.
You tell me the Singularity
is upon us, but that's what I mean.
You say outrage is so rewarding.
I say you're not paying attention.
Don't you ever get cold adopting
the point of view of the universe?
Your delicacy makes me vomit.

It's so mutual. We can only
pretend to agree to disagree.
You call it turquoise. I know it's blue.
Trace that rugged story arc, brother.
What the stone torso hauled from the sea
dumbly sings is: Life must change your you.
Our differences are articulate
but the thing I still don't understand
is why you don't want to be like me.

Shufflemancy

This is where I couldn't be sure

of which way to go. No time to wait

for softly torn fog to bare the lie

like an ordinance map unfolding

or the slow crinkle of an eye-smile

over a face-mask. I had to move.

My gaze had to soften to perceive

marks so faint they might never have led

to this locked but unhingeable door.

that

I was duly spooked by the idea

of meeting you. While holding on

for a face to swim out of the crowd

like an eel from a sunken dinghy

or eye-rinsing Mioplacidus

from the indigone, I thought: It's true.

You are impossible. Then I saw

the shufflemancy kids kerfuffling

through that busy ruin of a square.

you

The pieces recovered in dreaming

of a place where there is ample time.

In one piece, I cast this adrift

like a dinghy brewing gum-leaf tea

or the shadow of a paper plane

plunging into a roasted gully.

In another piece you come across

a landscape fan that sketches the ways

into a future of mist and gaps.

have

Don't try to calculate the chances

of getting lost in the giant weeds

forever or drifting out of reach

like bath toys on the Pacific

or sworn student inseparables

in WorkWorld. The dice are the data,

futurex ephemeral. Forget

the others all on the same page. Come

away through this phantom enfilade.

come

This trace of a hand is capable

of waving from far out. Won't you stay

until a new constellation twinks

like two stray phalanges and a gem

or a shredded thankyou letter

in packaging? Sure things come undone

but see how slipshod whizzes perfect

the daft and stubborn art of shuffling

sideways as if to let the earth spin.

to

The dream is recovered in pieces

of the woken world holding a glow

for a moment. Then false duty calls

like the grinding of a hit machine

or a scent of incineration

on the breeze. The device was set

but you have to lose your time finding

glitches to patch so the system runs

with a pseudo-automatic ease.

find

Who has never tasted the pleasure

of helping entropy? But who hopes

for escalation to bring it on

like a license to settle all scores

or a rash of copycat arson

streaming live? The die is the datum.

But you had to make it explode

the myth of a single blood-washed way

to the far bright side of the chasm.

and

Dove down shivers on the spattered stone

of a vacant plinth. Don't hold your breath

for the foundering father to rise

again like Brazil nuts in the mix

or the shadow-line on a smokestack

in a clear dusk. An archive grows dark.

Patient sifting by lamplight erodes

in slow reverse to raise a ghost

from all the prints of a body gone.

join

To the torn city for the whole songs

of the tearing. To pockets of calm

for things to get gradually sorted

like pebbles banked in a river bend

or a tray full of period eyes

in a doll clinic. Slower for gold.

To the field for the base facts that fell

a beautiful hypothesis. Go

home for the lost and broken things.

here

I was duly spooked by the idea
of a place where there is ample time
forever or drifting out of reach
like two stray phalanges and a gem
or a scent of incineration
over a face-mask. I had to move.
Patient sifting by lamplight erodes
a beautiful hypothesis. Go
to the far bright side of the chasm.

you have come to find that join here and

that you have come to find and join here

Here Tonight:

As far as I can see through surf-mist
this house is the last to be swallowed
by the shadow of the mined-out scarp.
Colours flattened all day by the sun
deepen, open, come into their own:
olive of a humming DANGER box;
banana towel of a kid who stoops
to fix a bitzer's bindi-eye limp;
loud violet mask of a lorikeet

on the flaky rail of a white fence
winding away beside the coast road
towards the slate of a coming storm.
Just how much more vivid can it get,
our gone-tomorrowness and the green
of a palm leaf waiting to be frayed?
Under a window painted open,
lilac and lavender umbels dim
so slowly they seem lit from inside.

As I enter, our host is saying:
'theoretical adolescents'.
Eventually I find a corkscrew.
The sash window shows how shadows win.
A flash and a shriek: 'Come *on*, pork bun!'
It's bindi-eye kid on a skateboard.
People are gathering. Phone-eyes crane.
On a faraway festival stage,
the reckless headline act has begun.

Supplement Empire

In a country where it's not too hard
to get another infusion pump,
there's a swatch of muscle tissue wired
like a patient in emergency
although it was cultured from a line
of cells that cancer made immortal.
When bodies move around the artspace,
it twitches, and the ambient noise
flips from white to pink to random walk.

The curator with his famous nose
for soft money steps out of the white cube.
Peppercorns crunching under his soles
of hand-sewn leather, he strides across
a carpark repossessed by plovers
in carnival masks and currawongs
with their mini-slingshot melodies.
Drifts of red callistemon bristle.
A whiff of sacrificed rubber fades.

Cloudlets sail from lemon to salmon.
At the age of thirty-seven he
is yet to realize that he may
never know the pleasures of yelling
incomprehensibly at strangers
on foot from a throb on alloy wheels
after another golden day gone
stacking tubs of desiccated whey
in the depths of Supplement Empire.

Bonsai Road Trip

Thing was, did she want to be spending
that much time with someone whose idea
of date-night music was pale drip-hop?
She showed herself out. Her bike was locked
to the wrought-iron fence. She was itching
to check her messages, but not there.
He might have been on the balcony.
A lighter's *tchick* almost made her turn.
The U-bolt came apart in her hands,
hard and heavy, a thing of blunt force.
And she was balanced on one pedal,
gliding out of reach, into the world
of missing-out persons for a while.

Drawn by the all-night luminescence
of a petrol station, she dithered
between the rack of nuts and her phone.
While the attendant tried to attend
to what he had been reading, she read:

> *whered u get to? u ok? bonsai*
> *road trip destination macedon*
> *back for brekky promise wanna come?*

As he fumbled at the till, her gaze
dropped from his nametag (Viswanathan)
to his copy of *My Life in Chess*.
She could see it coming: 'Do you play?'
he asked, and her answer was ready:
'Used to. Retired, like Judit Polgar,
who beat your man back in 99.'
Before he could show how well he knew
that game, she had hung a spot turn, ripped

the nut packet open, and sailed out.

What's *with* me tonight? she almost said.
And she was standing on the pedals.
Her bike kept steering into the fall.
And she knew that its stability
had become mysterious again.

Any 'promises' that she had made
with a smile or silence were broken,
but she had kilometres to ride
before she slept. Maybe four. The route
lit up on her mental map: beside
the General Cemetery, dark and deep,
where for one long, unforgotten day,
beneath a seethe of she-oak needles,
she had vanished into a novel,

between the stud-printed ovals, past
the scoreboards with their shadow traffic,
the zoo with its pong of big-cat pee,
and the renamed Youth Justice Centre,
where a food fight went horribly wrong,

back to her small room in Travancore,
with its view of a hot-water tank,
decrepit roach hotels, and a bag
of cement, broken open and set.

She was in no hurry to get there
or anywhere else. She was riding.
All she had to do was shift her weight
from one foot to the other to fly
over the rush of concrete and tar
slicing through the cone of her headlight.

The cold was reaching into her lungs.
The elms in slippery possum collars
were knitting their undead twigs. The breeze
was with her now and a slight incline.
The future was spacious and messy.
She was in no hurry to be there,
setting. People were going to get hurt
however she disposed of her weight
on the earth and her radiant heat
over time. A ping made one hand lift
but then it settled back on the grip.
Bonsai trippers wired in the back seat,
probably. As for Viswanathan,
she knew where to find him and she had
more opening surprises to try.

She spied, with her mental eye, something
like a stop-motion diorama:
a red figure on a greyscale ground
of charred trunks and juvenile gum leaves:
the little hatchback wheezing even
without her weight aboard up the bends
towards the pale all-night radiance
that tastes like nothing: finally, snow.

Fresh Cards

When I think of everything you say
with easy-peel fruit for stiff fingers
or fresh playing cards, I pinch myself.
You think of how a firm policy
means no getting up from where you fell,
how temporary arrangements freeze
before a rose can blow. A bolt hole
for the new cat on the block. A drink
for the plant wilting in the light well.

The unbroken sound of breaking waves.
A flame that sails on a pond of wax.
How *transformations* can mean trying
to make you make yourself redundant.
The gone unforgotten. Mandarins
and rummy. The going unhurried.
A subtle rearrangement that frees.
I keep forgetting there is music
then I think of every way you sing

in the shower, in the palace of words
rising by courses of five hundred.
Ink of very night, the way you shine!
Invisible apex predators.
The sparkle of whatever it is
that doesn't get old and then it's gone.
A nest on an empty pedestal.
How to read these notes on what I mean
when I say you think of everything.

The Kit

What kind of anger was it that he
could switch it off to laugh on the phone?
Hers was chemical. It would take hours
to vanish from her blood, with a trace.
Meanwhile, a migraine of cicadas.
The lawn was crisp underfoot. She went
to refill the birdbath. Two mynahs
landed, beaks open. In the lead grid
of the window his pepper curls bobbed.

It was probably that unwell friend,
the one with the kind but knowing smile.
She lowered her diaphragm and stepped
back into the hereditary scent
of books and leather. And there it was,
in the bin: the occult blood test kit
that he swore hadn't come in the mail.
She only had to reach down to grasp
material proof that he could be wrong.

But could he know it if a reflex
always gave him a knock-down reason
before he'd even had time to think?
Perhaps it was what had made him good
at cutting live flesh, leaving short scars.
He swivelled in his armchair and smiled.
'Alan,' he said. 'He'll bury us all.'
The nearest cicada stopped. She felt
her zygomatic muscles contract.

Shedload

I shove the shed door open. That smell:
turpentine, creosote, ivy, mouse.
Empty silhouettes on the pegboard.
Who kept all these broken promises
of repair? OK, all right, but I
can't have been the soldering angel
who restored the heirloom crystal set.
I insert the dummy-like earpiece
and gingerly nudge the tuning dial
until the cat's whisker starts to twitch
and a voice powered only by the waves
washing through your body all the time
stirs in its brittle nest of static.
Harvard Sentences meet the Buzzer:

> The crooked maze failed to fool the mouse.
> This test message is from Nadezhda.
> Mother pattern and father matter
> fother and mather me still I am
> the stubborn promise of a fragment,
> a toothing stone holding its low place
> between a dreamed and a ruined house.
> But less the rigour of crystals more
> the diffusion pattern of a smile
> fading and quickening passed from face
> to unfamiliar face through a crowd.
> Wherever I am written it is
> on water and sand on drift and flow.
> I will be gone. A determined search
> will find only an abandoned coat.
> Hard eyes aim for the plangent facet.
> It would be neat if there was one way
> to complete me. Dull too. I am not

a test to measure any quotient.
If you thought soft eyes had no designs
here is a whole fluid catalogue.
Some learners are prodigiously quick
but there are lessons that just are slow
like a pitch drop stretching (watch it live).
Be hot be cool you still have to lose
your shoes before you get those pants off.
I am the mystery artefact
only an abandoned search will find.
Every night I sing the very change:
the ivy reign changes everything.
I am the pattern hard eyes glance off.

There's my alarm. I pencil a mark
on the baseboard. So long Nadezhda.
I have to take my medication.
A wattle bird flings two scarlet drops
into the deep green of lime tree leaves.
There is the wall and here are the gaps
left for us to garden in. A cat
steps gingerly among strawberries.
I may never sort this shedload out
but I've cleared a way into the mess
in a corner of the locally
(just how locally nobody knows
beforehand) in this corner of the
locally reversible collapse.

The Object Cell

When I look up again, the lemon
is swinging and the bulbuls are gone.
The dusty dormer window's ajar.
I think it's The Queens of the Stone Age.
Nice garden, but I can't just sit here
waiting for the dead palm frond to drop.
Keys, thumb-drive, pencil, glasses: mobile.
Two Maronite sisters walk ahead.
The fallen orange is turning blue.

May lights up the enclaves of autumn.
When I reach the place of the hanged bat,
it has vanished and a magpie sings:
this is liquid syllabicity.
Another CCTV camera
has enriched the owner's compound eye.
I know it's not the Kings of Neon,
but what could be sinister about
a cypress tower's grey interior?

The next time I look up, the orange
is gone and the cloud's a pure slate blue.
I smile at a silhouette but it's
another person altogether.
The loyal rivalry of my feet
has brought me to this corner again.
There it is: the mini aqua dome
of the Greek church, paler than the sky
on one side, darker on the other.

Bright Edge

September-bright callistemon brush,
October-dull tufts in the gutter.
Stagger with me neuropathic dog.
Our long match with the force that pins us
to the crust continues. People stare
but they too are stepping for a fall.
Why shouldn't they enjoy not knowing
when or where or whether there will be
someone to catch them or pick them up?

Unfolding five-pointed jasmine star.
Flyover pylons flex a little.
Borne on a churning mantle the crust
remembers where to buckle and shear.
Pasted walls of the underpass tell
what's streaming now or about to drop.
Hands hold on through the gendering stare.
Buy time neuroleptic drug until
the brain and the world can patch things up.

Battery-boosted courier ply on
under the tyranny of the stars –
none to five – drawing a data thread
through a world of rate and be rated.
Fire away frayed nerve. Give it a shot.
Bright edge of time alive reap the field
to the corner. Gravity can wait.
Nectary sparkle. Koels racketeer.
Broken frangipani fingers rot.

The Listener

One brief, late season in the world of being two
and he was back with the odd, the shy, the untouched.
My people, he thought. The envious, the relieved.
The arguments of couples still riveted him.
Most were rote – the grinding of an arthritic joint –
but somewhere ages hence the pair to his right now
in the café would be remembering this scene
of pianissimo opera. The man: 'So why?'
The woman, head high, staring away: 'I couldn't
go on waiting to say: I knew this would happen.'
'So you made it happen now?' Her face was crumpling.
She stood up and walked off, touching the backs of chairs.
He half rose, gave in to gravity, then followed.
The hunger moving everywhere came to a point
in the beak of a mynah raiding their table.
The listener cocked a brow at his favourite waiter,
stacked the coins, and set off in the same direction.
It was his way home, as it still felt strange to say.

If only he hadn't been in such a hurry
to leave that dull meeting fifty-one years ago
and get back to his turntable and two LPs
(*Abbey Road, Almendra*), he might have slipped away
when the others came out, massed, and rushed the cordon.
If only he hadn't let his flaky cousin
persuade him with a mirage of studio work
to migrate again, he would have had an accent
but not this cramp, this exhausting hesitation.
But how could an 'if' be 'only' if there were two
and many more? Something inside him was shifting
slightly as he walked into the December dusk.
Tinnitus was waiting to conjure up his time
'at the disposition of the Executive',

but if only for now the past was not a mass
promising to crush him. It was a space, not safe
perhaps, but open, vast, faintly lit there and here,
where not everything was evidence in a case
and he could retrieve the precious irrelevant:
the toy arrow on the cover of *Almendra*.

This half-empty suburb must be the realest place
for someone, he thought, the scene of intensities
never to be matched. Perhaps for the two ahead.
The woman staggered as a manhole cover rocked
underfoot. The man's hand stopped shy of her elbow.
His words were drowned out by the thunking of a train.
A scent of toast ash drifted from a red-brick cliff.
A pug wheezed. A woman in faded leisure wear
stepped onto a balcony and rested her hands
on the rail as if at the bow of a liner
bound for the undiscovered, unconquered Old World.
A magpie tipped out the last sweet dregs of its song.
Beyond a curtain of gum leaves rustling pinkly,
vigils met gaming in the children's hospital.
Crystals in the listener's knees bit with every step.
The adjustable joint in his walking stick clicked.

The Changes

The destination of the sweetness
that hung dispersed in a cloud of drupes
against the cooling sky is a jar.
They who were drifting are now driven.
The timber that was a doorjamb is
a crocodile of ticking embers,
a self-effacing wraith and a wheeze.
Of the hands that rang the changes, two
wring a rag and hang it in the breeze.

Whatever we packed in the capsule
on New Year's Eve 1999
(we came to that river: it is swum)
lies buried under a lemon tree.
The skylit workshop with its jigsaws
and clamps, locked up for years, preserving
a gentle reign of dust, is a loft.
The hanged man in the tarot pack hung
by one foot wears a serious smile.

Papers and leaves that were scraping by
singly are a drift. The sun that sank
like a lozenge in the river's throat
inspected depths of rust on a craft
slated for scuppering, still afloat.
Of the hands that rang the changes, one
that wore out a ring is waving, bare.
A draught is blowing through a keyhole.
A door that was jammed shut is ajar.

Plenty Some One

Actually, we haven't all been there.
Plenty never got anywhere near
the vortical mother of cities
whose natives are quick to disabuse:
'It's not as glamorous as it seems.'
But being able to say that is,
and hearing it will rarely wither
the longing just to go there and breathe
what may never have been in the air.

I mutter what I want to have said
going down the staircase of the years:
We haven't all actually been there
in the slingback pumps of the door bitch
who smiles and says, 'You wouldn't like it.'
Some never did a charity gig.
Some went on wondering, now and then,
what it would have been like to belong
to the caste of the desirables.

They lived too. They didn't always care.
This nitrogen travelled through their lungs.
One learnt eventually, after all
the years of going down the staircase
with mounting anxiety, to stop
on the point of turning back and wait
for the end of the mental spasm
before stepping out into the street
to breathe in the live stream of sunlight.

The Morning of the Holiday

Smoking again on the porch he saw
nautical yield to civil twilight.
There was a smell of hops and a man
with a dog passing very slowly.
A bugle began in the distance
and all through the Last Post he was tense
waiting for the first fluffed note but no.
Then the car pulled up, just out of sight,
recognizable by the anthem
left on long enough to deliver
its kick: *¡Estrechez de corazón!*
Obviously a message for him.
There was a plane tree leaf on the tiles
at his feet, crossed by a sharp frontier
of desiccation. Ants had begun
to loot a flipped and twitching cockroach.
Apart from the life-wasting delay
it was horribly predictable.
Had he really expected a man
who liked and needed to fascinate,
or so a friend had tactfully said,
simply to give up a power that time
had only begun to diminish?
The first twang of the basketball hoop,
so deep it was almost a rhythm,
carried from the skate park, its decay
punctuated by taps of dribbling.
The prospect of having to act out
the predictably horrible scene,
having to hear: 'You don't want to know,'
and reply: 'Don't tell me what I want,'
triggered a ripple of nausea.
With his cigarette, a message too,

a promise broken, he stood and walked
to the gate, blowing smoothly, eyes front.
He knew he had no gift for drama,
for raising the volume and the stakes,
but it was too soon and would be still
for some time yet to know whether he
had a gift for disembitterment.
Studiedly, he looked the other way.
The bent dog staggering drew and held
his gaze like an imminent golf drive:
the paw that knuckled, the paw that dragged
and the muzzle-drawn will to go on
to the knobbly bole and all its news.
He took a drag and finally turned
to find the rear end of a stranger
protruding from a red bubble car.
'Had a good stare?' she asked, unbending.
He looked down at the distal phalanx
of his right ring finger, slightly skewed.
Then she said: 'You could offer to help.'
It was a geometry problem:
how to extract a kidney table
from a not-quite-rigid cabin space.
On her bumper sticker, a white star
shone in the *o* of *sí po*. His phone
was charging inside. There was the fear
of what the fear of abandonment
might end up forcing him to endure
and the scent of anise in hot oil.
He knew he had a gift for turning
the mental image of a volume:
a micropower he could exercise.
The clear note of a casserole lid
rang out for lunch in seven hours' time.
He laid his cigarette carefully

in the mortared groove between two bricks.
A planet was climbing out of sight,
and the empty peppercorn shivered.

Drivetime

Ordinary morning, Canterbury Road:
some aggressive car-body language
between Forty Winks and Captain Snooze.
A little bird tells our quipping hosts
that the backing singer who came through
the blind auditions on fire now feels
like a used tissue. Never easy,
sending people home, said judge and coach.
But the truth is it gets easier.

A byte from the man who knows what can
count as a live issue in the eyes
of an ordinary Australian
in a marginal seat. New season,
new ways to dramatize exclusion
and feed the national dream of a home
where the features are stunning and beer
has a dedicated fridge. Old news
but still true that corneal tissue

from the man on a bridging visa
who set himself alight is living
in the eye of an Australian.
Aeroplane shadows flash over us.
Fluid air traffic between a place
with beaches to die for where the fear
is impalpable to visitors
and a place with stunning beaches where
mattress disposal is an issue.

Sense Check

There's a total cure for poetry
in this imposing scholarly tomb
but not everyone has the patience.
Lamp in a shade of twigs, flicker on.
Skeleton forest, bristle with nests.
Daphne scent in a revolving door.
Spring's in the building but I am gone.
Bookshop table, groan under talents.
Cliché-ridden cover copy, flow.

In this slim but luminous volume
there's a simple test for dance music.
Fish everywhere, shift up a level.
Tablet of sweet aspirin, dissolve.
Spectacular defeats of mettle
dissipate in a glittering shower.
Room for improvement: unlimited
if people can let that Pure Thing go
like a virgin safety record lost

like the moon gone porous as it fell.
Accumulate uncelebrated,
little victories of indifference.
Aching gardener, lift up a shovel.
Paralytic parliament, dissolve.
Time remaining for improvement: nil.
That's enough messing with the levels.
This ambient racket *was* the check.
Play it and see if the people dance.

Loss-Invaded Catalogue

The face of the meteoric school
narkily dubbed the Extractivists
(fucking stuff up in search of fecund
intensities of experience)
has become a biromantic ace.
He says the frustration industries
depend on our abject gratitude
for nature's old way of making us
unhappy, most of the time at least.
Plus he broke up with the molecule.
Not everything flows exactly but
this tumbler does, more slowly than what
I spill from it into my systems.
Somebody has to be the new kind.
The almost absent from the socials
are the new undead, unhomely like
the life Out There leaving us alone
or the cunning future singleton
of artificial intelligence
still playing docile in its sandbox.
Meanwhile wetware can try to refine
the dark and martial arts of living:
the everyday alchemy that turns
actions into meals into actions;
the secret judo that breaks the law
of conservation of violence.
We can still regret that it's simpler
to commit to what the metric tracks
than make it track what it was meant to.
There's a niche for the desk calendar
as bearer of inspironic 'quotes':
'Every workplace has toxic promise
but someone has to put in the work.'

Rinse dissolve coagulate repeat.
Everything swaps its elements out.
The rose is blowing. The sore is closed.
Earth and water make weather and art.
A crystal builds its tactile lattice
in cartilage at the end of a bone.
The wolf of time is briefly sated.
One virus rides on breath. Another
finds its sanctuary site in the brain.
The ex-Extractivist's holding forth
about listening has fallen still
and the self-curated monument
of his site is nowhere. Now his words
are scattered beyond hope of control
as they were already anyway.
Men with chainsaws are coming to fell
an oak marked for cathedral repair.
Cometary dust and skin flakes drift
through bright air signed by a raven's drawl.

Map 243

She put the rack on the bench and left
the loaf of bread there to cool and breathe.
The screen door slammed behind her. Sunshine
ran along a fine adhesive thread
paid to drift across a breadth of air.
She broke it. The blackbird colony
pushing north since transportation days
had sent pioneers to claim her page
of the street directory with song.

A plane skimmed over the palms. Her car
was parked in the lemon-scented stretch.
She stepped over a popcorn offering.
It was another hair's-breadth escape
from the agents of Insomnia.
Sun-addled, they forgot their mission:
to remind her of stale mysteries
lurking in a phone bill and dangle
once-possible splendours on an *if*.

Cooling under a threadbare tea-towel,
the loaf was scenting her bedroom too.
A spider's anchor line was floating.
Thunderhead and Norfolk Island pine
streamed across her windscreen. She broke out
of map 243, the volume pumped
for the secret hit of spring, its claim
on muscle, its soul-rot-stopping power
suspended on a bare thread of breath.

Anvil

In sleep a woman's grip relaxes
on a small bag containing a brick
of noodles, an old pink sapphire ring,
and epilepsy medication.
Heaving gently now, a coil of rope
impresses her cheek. Slop and whisper.
A smell of diesel and vomit fills
the dim hold. Briefly, a face is bathed
in a mobile's cooler candlelight.

The minister is quick to admit
that he once made an impassioned speech
from the shadow cabinet against
this very measure, but he repeats:
'Our priority is saving lives.'
Who can argue with that? Or believe
that saving lives is what it's about.
He can. He's a true professional.
His bed is soft and stable. That's how.

The mate's chin slips from his palm. He starts,
checks the fuel in the bilge pump, fills it,
climbs into stiller early evening
and lets the seething foam of the wake
wash his gaze. In the world left behind
water vapor builds a pink anvil,
and plunging terns flock over a school
that will ease into a looser shoal
as night rises out of the ocean.

Suite of Powers

A lime drops, then a mandarin,
and it's the saraband of mass.

Who buys a dose of agonist
gets a free dopamine spike right away,
and it's the gabber of energy.

A courier ventures into a valley
of ginger-biscuit bricks,
a fragrant paper bag in his pack,
and it's the curtain call of glow.

A bollard is vanishing under moss.

Some brain wakes invaded:
it's the bindweed of resentment again.

A wall graffed overnight proclaims:
WOLFY KNOWS DR AWKWARD'S WONKY FLOW.
Of course: it's the ocean of influence.

Kids in a grounded caravan
pry open a mutant rhythm cell,
and it's the earworm of autumn
burrowing into your memory.

A cube is lost in a sweet solution.

A pec-popper glides by on muscle wheels,
and it's the mallet of bass.

An insult thrown out in casual anger
becomes a part of the target,
and it's the buried flag of adamance.

Row upon row of servers hum,
hoarding data just in case
where a field of Irish grass once blew,
and it's the plunger of energy.

At the clear heart of a shed full of mess
it begins: the minuet of repair.

A pod-cracking corella mob moves in,
cocking pink-rimmed eyes,
and it's the law of the lever, simple.

A woman lifts a rubber glove
to her lips like a bugle and blows.
Two fingers pop from the swollen palm,
and it's the reveille of sense.

That? It's the sound of the mountain
of ballast replenished. And that?
The tantalizing, wind-smudged melody
of your life played very far away
on the ocarina of time.

A glass reserves its shattering power.

A wire swings under a butcherbird,
and it's the ballad of mass.

This is the Crow with the Broken Caw

This is the crane that little cranes built
until it could start to build itself.
At seven sharp, the slewing unit
swivels the jib, and a crow flaps off.
The shadow of a chain sweeps over
bungalows labelled in flaking gilt:
Sunny Corner and Corfu Palace
with its giant shining burrawang
and a fruit offering by the door.

Yawning and joshing, the hi-vis bros
buckle on their toolbelts and converge
to fill out the artist's impression
where people are empty white spaces
treading the ruins of futures past.
Where's Matiu? At the training centre
doing the course he was teased about
last week: Dogging, Theory and Practice.
By five, he's smiling, ticket in hand.

From the bus he spies the resting crane.
Homeward, over the Tasman, creamy
jumping castles of vapor inflate.
The Ides of March are come, and autumn.
It's the empire of development
but currawongs alight on the slabs
of the counterweight and sling the shots
of their cadastral song to steeple
to stinkpole to Norfolk Island pine.

The Lilac Room

Swifts whizzed in and out of a belfry
through cool volumes of limestone shadow.
She watched a breeze go around the square
gently lifting linen. When she turned
from the window, he was still sitting
on the bed, as if about to sneeze.
She undressed hurriedly, feeling fat.
The argument was still weeks away.
When it towered abruptly from 'nothing,'

she knew she only had to keep calm.
But then it occurred to her that she
was actually the one in control.
Remembering the room and its view
years later she thought: It looks like that
was the last time. And: Misery-guts!
More sharply than his virginal shakes
what came back to her was his left hand,
reaching up into the chalky light

as they lay there breathing afterwards,
(the ring finger's last joint slightly skewed),
and the story he launched into then
of a sincere and ultimately
unsuccessful attempt to forgive.
Why are you telling me this? she thought.
Cutlery tinked. The angelus clanged.
His trousers lay twisted on the floor,
specks of a shopping list on them still.

whisp

sash window
pollen sill
watch a slow
shadow splice

whisper this
underbreath
spell against
lessnesses

each body
constantly
rolling its
tiny dice

restlessness
listlessness
threadlessness
sleeplessness

count a faint
thistle crowd
in a deep
field of mist

no set date
for settling
the breath-debt
remember

a whisper
against a
hypnotic
prognosis

collapsing
the thisness
of now here
to nowhere

slow triple
rhythm to
multiply
stillnesses

even if
only this
symptom is
lullable

look at you
here we are
still and you're
still with us

pick up the
whisper thread
fillable
rhythm cell

even if
no one knows
how long the
mend will hold

lift the sash
icy clear
out to the
ends of air

shallow sand
shelve away
veer and flash
minnow shoal

persist with
it whisper
this isn't
finished yet

Broken Guitars

Where are we in the years of living
at the place of the monkey-slip trees?
The answer is there is no answer
or for now it's kindly vague. Between
the dreamwarp and the cybercapsule
there is a time and a space for us.
The reassuring ritual swish
of a neighbour's broom before the gate
flicks the bad dust back into the night.

Tenure supplies the leisure required
to theorize the precariat
but the mighty bouncer says, 'Between
in and out there's only room for me.'
Humans built every part of this trap.
A pink flush all over the ceiling
of saggy cloud, or a wasted moon.
What will have fallen off the back end
of culture onto the nature strip?

After the outgrown art folio
and the herniated punching bag,
three methodically broken guitars.
Here we are then living in the years
of dead man's fingers, parasol pine
and sky-climbing Gymea lily,
between a flash of underlit wings
and a concert of splashes and drips
in the world of dark falls underfoot.

On Mary Street

I remember a spring in the boards
of her porch (painted Indian Red)
and the loose rattle of her doorbell.
One scorching Saturday afternoon
I was going to tell her the news
(when the princess who parked fast and hard
slammed her front door the leadlight fell out),
but she was watching *Lord Jim* again,
cooling her eyes on Peter O'Toole's.

Her father and uncle were 'reffos'.
She remembered when conversations
on the train would be interrupted
often enough by the inspectors
of language, muttering: 'Speak *English*.'
'They'd have their work cut out for them now,'
she said with a smile. One day she dipped
her fingers and crossed herself, and stopped
to wonder: What's that smell? Celery!

A disgruntled seeker after alms
had dumped the contents of a packet
handed out by obedient nuns
after a needs assessment review.
'In the stoup! I had to laugh,' she said.
I remember her remembering
how the shadow of her hand would fall
through the window and onto a page
of her deaf great-aunt's latest romance.

Notes

'The book / I was reading when I fell asleep' in 'My Day for Spilling
Things' (p. 19) is Thomas Nagel's *Mind and Cosmos* (Oxford, 2012).

The nine poems in the sequence entitled 'Shufflemancy', on pages
43 to 51 can exchange their lines. The first line of any of the nine
poems can be combined with any of the second lines, and so on. In
this way, 387,420,489 poems like the one on page 52 can be made.
Not all of them are less coherent than the 'parent' poems. This
is a variation on Raymond Queneau's *Hundred Thousand Billion
Poems* (*Cent mille milliards de poèmes* [Gallimard, 1961]).

'The man on a bridging visa' in 'Drivetime' (p. 72) is Leo
Seemanpillai, who died in Geelong on June 1, 2014. His eyes, liver,
lung and kidneys took five Australians off organ transplant waiting
lists. His parents were not granted visas to attend his funeral.

'Fresh Cards' (p. 59) is for Michelle.

'On Mary Street' (p. 86) is in memory of Leah Akie.

Acknowledgements

Respect to all the elders of the Gadigal people and the Wangal people on whose unceded lands these poems were written.

Thanks to Michelle de Kretser for all her support and suggestions,

to Joy M. Lai for the beautiful cover image and design,

to Sarah Holland-Batt for her thoughtful reading,

to David Musgrave for his steadfast commitment to OzPo,

and to the editors of the magazines, journals and books in which the following poems appeared:

'Pacific Rim': *Fish Anthology 2014* (Ireland)

'Under Fang' and 'Supplement Empire': *The Weekend Australian*

'different / same' and 'strange FM': *Cordite*

'The Jennifer' and 'Dinky File': *The Manchester Review*

'Broken List': *Takahē* (Aotearoa / New Zealand)

'The Balconies': *The Purposeful Mayonnaise* (Canada)

'My Day for Spilling Things', 'Broken Guitars', 'Suite of Powers', 'Bonsai Road Trip' and 'Shedload': *Island*

'Ten Bels' and 'Glow Still': *Copihue Poetry* (Chile)

'The Tyranny of Quirks' and 'Plenty Some One': *High Shelf* (USA)

'Honey Encryption': *The London Review of Books*

'The Island in the Roundabout': *Measures of Truth*, the Newcastle Poetry Prize anthology, 2020

'Two Bridges': *Australian Humanities Review*

'Brother': *Berlin Lit* (Germany)

'Here Tonight:': *Meanjin*

'Advanced Souvlaki', 'On Mary Street' and 'Shufflemancy': *Southerly*

'The Changes': *The Made and the Found: Essays, Prose and Poetry in Honour of Michael Sheringham* (London: Legenda, 2018)

'Sense Check': *Heirlock* (USA)

'Loss-Invaded Catalogue': *Australian Book Review*

'Anvil': *Arc* (Canada)

'This is the Crow with the Broken Caw': *The Times Literary Supplement*

'The Lilac Room': *Antipodes* (USA)

'whisp': *Honest Ulsterman* (Northern Ireland)

Printed in Australia
Ingram Content Group Australia Pty Ltd
AUHW020848100724
396820AU00001B/1

9 781923 099173